How To Make Your Business Your Business

"Empowering Entrepreneurs: Building, Scaling, and Succeeding in Business"

GREEN WONDY

Contents

INTRODUCTION

Welcome to "How to Make Your Business Your Business," the definitive handbook for entrepreneurs who want to control their firm, define its future, and leave an everlasting imprint on the business world. This book is your road map to bringing your entrepreneurial vision, principles, and passion to life if you've ever wanted to create a company that does.

The path from simple existence to actual ownership in the broad and dynamic world of entrepreneurship is an exciting one, full of obstacles and victories. With more than ten years of practical experience under my belt, I am an experienced business owner who has seen the ups and downs of the industry and learned what it takes to not just survive but thrive. "How to Make Your Business Your Business" is more than simply a book—it's a guide, a mentor, and a manual for turning your company into an expression of your dreams.

The process starts with a thorough analysis of your company's identification. It's more important to focus on who you are and what makes you stand out than merely what you offer. We'll go into the subtleties of developing an engaging vision, a purpose that speaks to people, and a brand identity that sticks in their minds and hearts.

Establishing a strong base is the next essential stage. A company without a strong foundation is like a house of cards that is about to fall apart. We'll go into great detail in this part on how to build up your business structure, write a thorough business plan, and create goals that will help you succeed.

The foundation of long-term success is understanding finance. We'll walk you through the financial nuances that have the power to make or destroy your company, from budgeting to managing cash flow to making wise investments.

There are obstacles along the way, and surviving the legal and regulatory environments is essential to the journey's success. Discover how to manage risks, maintain compliance, and safeguard your intellectual property in a world where legal nuances can be just as complicated as your company.

However, a business is more than simply organizational structures and financial records—it's a group of people coming together to work toward a similar objective. Learn the exclusive tips for selecting and keeping top people, building a winning team, and producing inspiring leadership in the chapters on building a winning team.

We'll solve the puzzles of successful marketing and sales tactics, leveraging technology for expansion, and growing your company to success as we go along. This book is about leaving a legacy, not simply about starting a business.

So grab a seat; this will be an exciting ride. "How to Make Your Business Your Business" is your travel companion on the path to business ownership and success, regardless of whether you're just getting started or want to grow your current enterprise. Now let's get the journey started!

CHAPTER 1

BUILDING A SOLID FOUNDATION

Establishing Your Business Structure

A crucial first step in becoming an entrepreneur is creating a business structure, which sets the framework for your company's operations, legal responsibilities, and profit-sharing arrangements. This is a thorough how-to tutorial for creating a business structure:

1. Recognize Various Business Structures:

Learn about the several kinds of business forms that are out there, including corporations, partnerships, limited liability companies (LLCs), sole proprietorships, and cooperatives. Selecting a structure that fits your objectives, risk tolerance, and long-term aspirations is crucial since each one has pros, cons, and legal ramifications of its own.

2. Assess Your Objectives and Needs:

The optimum business structure for your needs, objectives, and priorities will be determined via assessment. Take into account elements like scalability, tax ramifications, liability protection, and management flexibility. A structure that is effective for a small, owner-operated company might not be appropriate for a high-growth, bigger enterprise.

4. Register Your Company:

After deciding on a business structure, you must register your company with the relevant government agencies. Usually, this entails paying registration fees, getting licenses and permissions, and completing documentation. The procedure differs depending on where you live and the kind of structure you select, so make sure to adhere to the particular guidelines provided by your local government.

5. Draft Legal Documents:

Draft and carry out legal documents that establish the organization and procedures of your company. These might be the bylaws (for companies), operating agreements (for LLCs), partnership agreements (for partnerships), or articles of incorporation (for corporations). The rights, obligations, and connections between stakeholders and company owners are outlined in these papers.

6. Obtain Necessary Permits and Licenses:

In order to lawfully function, your business may require a number of licenses, permits, and certificates, depending on its location and type. These might include certificates unique to a certain sector, zoning permissions, health permits, company licenses, and professional licenses. To prevent future legal problems, learn about the rules that apply to your company and make sure that you are in compliance.

7. Maintain Compliance:

Remain aware of any upcoming legal requirements pertaining to the business structure you have selected. This might entail keeping up with taxes, filing yearly reports, keeping track of corporate documents, hosting shareholder meetings for firms, and abiding by industry-specific regulations. Penalties, fines, and legal ramifications may follow noncompliance with these duties.

Developing a Business Plan

Creating a thorough business plan is essential to defining your goals, providing ways to reach them, drawing in investors, and obtaining funding. The following rules should be adhered to while creating a business plan:

1. Executive Summary:

Give a succinct outline of your business concept, market potential, competitive advantage, financial predictions, and finance requirements in your executive summary. This part should draw the reader in and give a brief overview of the contents of the business plan.

2. Business Description:

Give a thorough overview of your company, outlining its objectives, values, vision, and mission. Describe your target market, the needs or problems your company seeks to solve, and the goods and services you provide. Emphasize the unique selling points of your company and the reasons why clients should select your products.

3. Market Analysis:

To fully comprehend your target market, industry, and competitive environment, do in-depth market research. Determine your target market's demographics, inclinations, and purchasing patterns. Examine market size, growth potential, the competitive landscape, and industry trends. To validate your company idea and support your analysis, use facts and statistics.

4. Sales and Marketing Plan:

Describe your strategy for attracting and keeping consumers in terms of sales and marketing. Identify your marketing channels, including networking, social media, digital advertising, and content marketing. Give specifics about your distribution routes, price plan, sales techniques, and promotional initiatives. Explain how you plan to set your brand apart from the competition and position it in the market.

5. Operations and Management:

Describe the day-to-day operations, management group, and organizational structure of your company. Outline your personnel needs and hiring strategy, as well as the roles and duties of important team members. Explain your facility's needs, supply chain management, and production process. Talk about any operational-related legal or regulatory issues.

6. Financial predictions:

Create thorough financial predictions, including balance sheets, cash flow statements, and income statements, for your company. For the following three to five years, anticipate your launch expenditures, ongoing costs, sales figures, and revenue. To support your financial projections, use data-driven research and reasonable assumptions. Incorporate milestones and key performance indicators (KPIs) to monitor advancement and assess achievement.

7. Requirements for Funding: Establish the amount of capital you'll need to start and expand your company, as well as your intended purpose for the money. Describe the sources of your finance, including loans, investors, crowdsourcing, and personal savings. Give a thorough explanation of your financial needs, taking into account working capital, capital expenditures, and contingency reserves. Make a convincing argument for why investors should fund your company.

8. Assessment and Mitigation of Risk:

Determine the risks and obstacles that could affect the success of your company and create plans to address them. Evaluate the risks associated with internal variables, competitive markets, changing regulations, and the state of the economy. Describe backup plans and risk-reduction techniques to deal with unforeseen circumstances and guarantee business continuity.

9. Appendices:

Provide any further study results, supporting papers, or other material that strengthens the validity and comprehensiveness of your business plan. Key team member resumes, market research papers, product prototypes, court records, and financial statements are a few examples of this.

Setting Clear Goals and Objectives

For your company's efforts to have direction, concentration, and purpose, you must set clear goals and objectives. Here are some pointers for creating goals and objectives that work:

1. Align with Your Vision and Mission:

Make sure your goals and objectives are in line with your company's overall vision and purpose. The fundamental principles, objectives, and long-term goals that propel your company forward have to be reflected in them.

2. Measure and specify yourself:

Give a clear explanation of your goals and objectives, including what you hope to accomplish and how success will be measured. To quantify your goals and monitor your progress over time, use precise metrics like revenue targets, market share, customer satisfaction scores, or key performance indicators (KPIs).

3. Set realistic and achievable targets:

Take into account the state of the market, your present resources, and your ability when setting tough but reachable goals. Strive for goals that push your boundaries and spur personal development, but also avoid establishing lofty objectives that might overwhelm or demoralize your team.

4. Order and Prioritize Objectives:

Establish the relative urgency and significance of each objective, then rank them in order of priority. Create a sensible plan for accomplishing your objectives, giving priority to those that will have the biggest effects on the performance of your company, or take care of urgent issues first.

5. Determine explicit timelines and benchmarks:

To instill a feeling of urgency and accountability, give each goal and aim clear dates and milestones. To keep things moving forward and monitor development gradually, break down more ambitious objectives into smaller, more doable tasks with intermediate deadlines.

6. Include Important Parties:

Involve important parties in the goal-setting process, such as staff members, managers, investors, and clients, to secure support, promote cooperation, and guarantee alignment with more general company goals. In order to provide a variety of viewpoints and thoughts, encourage participation, comments, and input.

7. Monitor and evaluate development regularly:

Put in place a strategy to continuously track and assess your goals' development. To stay on track and overcome hurdles, monitor pertinent metrics and performance indicators, carry out routine reviews and assessments, and make necessary adjustments to your strategy and tactics.

8. Celebrate Achievements and Learn from Setbacks:
To acknowledge advancement and inspire your team, celebrate little victories along the way. In a similar vein, reflect on your mistakes, setbacks, and departures from your original plan, draw lessons from them, and modify your strategy going forward.

9. Remain Adaptable and Flexible:

Maintain your adaptability and responsiveness to shifts in internal capabilities, market dynamics, and the business environment. As conditions change, be prepared to adjust your goals and objectives in order to take advantage of new possibilities and reduce potential hazards.

CHAPTER 2

MASTERING FINANCIAL MANAGEMENT

Budgeting and Financial Planning

Effective financial management in company relies heavily on budgeting and financial planning, which support businesses' strategic resource allocation, performance monitoring, and financial goal-achieving. Below is a description of each:

1. Budgeting:

Forecasting future revenue and costs, as well as assigning resources to various projects and activities within a company, are all part of the budgeting process. It acts as a financial road map that directs the distribution of resources, decision-making, and performance assessment. Important budgeting components include:

- **Revenue Forecasting:** Projecting future income streams from investments, sales, services, and other sources in order to calculate the total anticipated revenue for a certain time frame.

- **Expense Projectio:** Planning ahead and classifying projected costs, such as debt repayment, wages, operational costs, overhead, and raw materials.

- **Budget Allocation:** Determining the relative significance, priority, and projected returns of various departments, projects, or activities before allocating resources (e.g., cash, time, or staff).
- **Budgetary Controls:** Establishing controls over expenditure, including spending caps, authorization for certain expenses, variance analysis, and recurring budget reviews.
- **Budget Variance Analysis:** This involves comparing actual financial performance to projected numbers in order to find differences, assess the causes of the variations, and implement any necessary remedial measures.

Businesses benefit from budgeting:

Arrange and rank their expenses.
 - Assure effective and efficient utilization of available resources.
manage liquidity and predict future cash flow requirements.
Assess performance in relation to predetermined goals.
Make well-informed choices on the distribution of

resources, potential investments, and cost-reduction strategies.

2. Financial Planning:

The methodical process of evaluating the financial health of a business, establishing financial objectives, and creating plans to reach those objectives is known as financial planning. It is more comprehensive than budgeting and emphasizes risk management, long-term financial development, and sustainability. Important financial planning components include:

- **Goal Setting:** Establishing quantifiable, precise financial goals in line with the purpose, vision, and strategic priorities of the company.

- **Risk Assessment and Management:** recognizing possible financial risks and uncertainties (such as credit, market, and operational risks) and creating plans to reduce or successfully manage them.

- **Investment Planning:** Assessing financing choices, capital projects, and investment possibilities in order to maximize profits, cut expenses, and promote expansion plans.

Cash Flow Management: Keeping an eye on working capital, liquidity, and cash flows to make sure the company stays solvent and can pay its short-term debts.

- **Tax planning:** maximizing tax obligations by utilizing legitimate methods of tax reduction, credits, deductions, and regulatory compliance.

- **Retirement and Succession Planning:** Making preparations for important stakeholders' long-term financial stability, such as owners, executives, and staff, through pension plans, retirement savings, and succession plans.

Managing Cash Flow Effectively

Effective cash flow management is essential to a company's stability and financial health. Monitoring, predicting, and optimizing the movement of cash into and out of the company are all part of cash flow management, which aims to keep the company's liquidity sufficient to pay short-term debts and maintain operations. The following are some methods for efficiently handling cash flow:

1. Establish a Cash Flow forecast:

Create a cash flow projection that estimates your anticipated inflows and outflows of funds over a given time frame, usually on a quarterly or monthly basis. To precisely anticipate your future financial condition, use historical data, sales projections, spending forecasts, and other pertinent information.

2. Regularly Monitor Cash Flow:

Examine your cash flow statement frequently to keep tabs on real cash inflows and outflows in comparison to your projected amounts. Find any differences or inconsistencies, and look into the underlying causes. Frequent monitoring enables you to see any financial surpluses or shortfalls early on and take proactive steps to resolve them.

3. Optimize Accounts Receivable:

Quickly increase the amount of money collected from unpaid invoices by putting in place effective invoicing procedures, providing early payment discounts, and following up on past-due invoices. To reduce the risk of bad debts, establish explicit credit standards, assess consumers' credit, and agree on reasonable payment conditions.

4. Manage Accounts Payable:

By negotiating longer payment terms or taking advantage of early payment discounts, you can postpone payments to vendors and suppliers without endangering your relationships. Sort payments into priority lists according to due dates and available funds to maximize your financial flow.

5. Control running expenses:

Keep a close eye on your running expenses and look for ways to cut back without compromising effectiveness or quality. Implement cost-cutting strategies such as contract renegotiation, supplier consolidation, outsourcing non-core operations, and cutting back on wasteful spending.

6. Maintain Adequate Working Capital:

Make sure your company has enough working capital on hand to pay for regular operating costs like payroll, rent, utilities, and inventory purchases. Keep a reserve of cash on hand or have access to a credit line in case of emergencies or unanticipated changes in cash flow.

7. Manage Inventory Levels:

To cut down on carrying expenses, get rid of extra inventory, and increase inventory turnover, streamline your inventory management procedures. Adopt just-in-time (JIT) inventory systems, make precise demand forecasts, and rank inventory goods according to turnover rates and profitability.

8. Maximize Cash Inflows:

Look into ways to boost your cash inflows by offering new products or services, growing into new markets, conducting promotional campaigns, diversifying your income streams, or speeding up sales.

9. Utilize Cash Flow Management Tools:

To automate tedious work, improve cash flow efficiency, and learn more about your cash flow dynamics, make use of software and cash flow management tools. With the use of these tools, you may create cash flow estimates, monitor receivables and payables, and pinpoint areas that need improvement.

Investing Wisely in Your Business

Making prudent company investments is crucial to fostering innovation, development, and long-term success. Allocating resources strategically to areas that offer the best possible return on investment (ROI) and correspond with your business objectives is a key component of effective business investment. Here are some pointers to help you make prudent business investments:

1. Establish Your Investment Objectives:

Make a list of your top priorities and investment goals, such as growing your market share, boosting profits, increasing productivity, raising the caliber of your products, or breaking into new markets. Establish precise standards for assessing investment prospects and make sure they line up with your long-term goals and overarching business plan.

2. Conduct Thorough Due Diligence:

Evaluate the possible risks, benefits, and viability of any opportunity by doing thorough due diligence prior to making any investment decisions. Considerations include industry trends, market demand, competitive environment, financial feasibility, and possible return on investment. To make well-informed judgments, consult with specialists, compile pertinent information, and assess market conditions.

3. Prioritize Investments Based on ROI:

Give top priority to those that will best support your business priorities and strategic goals while also offering the largest possible return on investment. Examine each investment's expected financial impact, taking into account expected revenue generation, cost savings, productivity benefits, and potential for long-term growth. Concentrate on making investments that will help your company succeed overall and have an obvious route to profitability.

4. Diversify Your Investments: To disperse risk and optimize growth and innovation prospects, diversify your investment portfolio. Distribute resources across several departments within your company, including operations, marketing, technology, product development, and talent acquisition. Strike a balance between long-term investments that create durable competitive advantages and future growth prospects and short-term investments that produce benefits right away.

5. Invest in innovation and technology:

Provide funds for innovation projects, R&D campaigns, and technological updates that will strengthen your position in the market, promote long-term growth, and differentiate your offerings. Take advantage of new possibilities in your sector and remain ahead of the competition by embracing evolving technology, trends, and market upheavals.

6. Invest in Your People:

Acknowledge that your staff members are your most precious resource and make investments in their welfare, growth, and training. To draw and keep top talent, offer chances for skill development, leadership training, and career growth. Create an environment at work where innovation, teamwork, and employee involvement are valued and encouraged. This will increase output and help the company succeed.

7. Monitor and evaluate investment performance:

Put in place a method to keep an eye on and assess how well your assets are performing in comparison to predetermined benchmarks, objectives, and metrics. Keep tabs on financial measurements, qualitative assessments, and key performance indicators (KPIs) to evaluate the return on your investments and make informed decisions. To improve your investing strategy over time, evaluate investment results on a regular basis, make necessary strategy adjustments, and take lessons from both triumphs and failures.

8. Stay Agile and Adaptable:

Continue to be adaptable and sensitive to shifting consumer tastes, market conditions, and industry dynamics. As possibilities, risks, and new trends change, so should your investment strategy and objectives. Adopt a culture that values innovation, experimentation, and continual improvement to help your company grow and prosper in a changing and unpredictable landscape.

CHAPTER 3

NAVIGATING LEGAL AND REGULATORY CHALLENGES

Understanding Legal Requirements

Complying with the law, reducing risks, and shielding your company from lawsuits all depend on your understanding of the standards. Legal requirements encompass various laws, regulations, and obligations imposed by government authorities at the local, national, and international levels. Here's a helpful guide to understanding legal obligations in business:

1. Identify laws and regulations that apply:

Determine which laws, rules, and industry standards are pertinent to your company depending on its size, industry, location, and range of activities. Legal rules that are frequently encountered include those pertaining to business registration and licensing, taxation, employment law, data protection, intellectual property rights, health and safety, environmental compliance, and consumer protection.

3. Conduct legal audits and assessments:

To find possible areas of legal risk, non-compliance, or vulnerability within your company's activities, conduct legal audits and assessments on a regular basis. Examine agreements, policies, processes, and contracts to make sure they are current and compliant with the law. Evaluate your adherence to pertinent rules and regulations and take proactive steps and remedial action to rectify any gaps or inadequacies.

4. Remain Updated on Legal Developments:

Keep up with any changes to industry standards, rules, or regulations that could affect how your firm operates. Through legal periodicals, government websites, industry groups, and professional networks, keep an eye on legislative changes, regulatory revisions, court opinions, and industry trends. To remain up-to-date on new legal developments and compliance needs, sign up for newsletters, go to legal seminars, and communicate with legal professionals.

5. Educate Staff About Legal Compliance:

Inform and instruct your staff about their legal responsibilities and obligations inside the company. To raise understanding of pertinent laws and regulations, ethical standards, and compliance processes, offer training programs, workshops, and resources. To handle problems proactively and avoid legal conflicts or liabilities, promote open communication and the reporting of legal concerns or breaches.

6. Create Policies and Procedures for Compliance: Create thorough compliance rules, processes, and internal controls to make sure your company complies with ethical and legal obligations. Put your rules and procedures on paper, make sure staff members understand them, and use enforcement tools, audits, and routine monitoring to ensure compliance. Create an organizational culture that is centered on ethical behavior and compliance.

7. Preserve Precise Records and Records:

For everything pertaining to your firm, including contracts, licenses, permits, transactions, and regulatory filings, maintain accurate and current records and paperwork. Observe regulatory obligations and industry best practices when organizing files and archives. Maintain documents for the required length of time, and then safely destroy them when you're done with them to safeguard private data and reduce legal concerns.

Effective organizational stewardship and governance in business need compliance and risk management. Along with making sure that laws, rules, and ethical standards are followed, they entail recognizing, evaluating, managing, and monitoring risks. An explanation of risk management and compliance in business is provided below:

1. Ethical Management:

Organizations use compliance management procedures and practices to make sure they are operating within the bounds of relevant laws, rules, policies, and standards. It contains:

- **Legal and Regulatory Compliance:** Ensuring adherence to pertinent laws, rules, and industry standards that control how business is conducted. Examples of these include financial regulations, employment laws, environmental regulations, data protection laws, and consumer protection laws.

- **Policy and Procedure Compliance:** Creating and implementing internal codes of conduct, rules, and procedures that adhere to moral and legal obligations. ensuring that staff are aware of policies, keeping an eye on compliance, and taking appropriate action when infractions happen.

- **Risk Assessment and Compliance Audits:** To find any non-compliance areas, flaws, and vulnerabilities inside the company, risk assessments and compliance audits are conducted. evaluating the performance of current processes and controls and making necessary adjustments to increase compliance.

- **Training and Awareness:** Offering staff education, training, and awareness initiatives to deepen their comprehension of ethical standards, compliance regulations, and their roles and responsibilities in upholding compliance. encouraging honesty and compliance as a culture across the whole company.

- **Reporting and Monitoring:** Putting in place procedures, channels, and reporting mechanisms so that staff members may report alleged infractions or compliance breaches. In order to successfully handle non-compliance, timely reporting of occurrences, monitoring, investigation, and appropriate disciplinary or remedial action are required.

2. Mitigation of Risk:

Identification, evaluation, prioritization, and mitigation of risks that might jeopardize the accomplishment of corporate goals are all part of risk management. It seeks to maximize chances for value generation while reducing the possibility and effect of unfavorable occurrences. Important facets of risk management consist of:

- **Risk Identification:** This involves recognizing and classifying potential hazards resulting from both internal and external sources. Examples of these risks include financial, operational, strategic, reputational, and market risks. carrying out risk assessments to determine each risk's likelihood and possible impact on corporate goals.

- **Risk Assessment and Analysis:** Applying quantitative and qualitative analysis tools to evaluate the likelihood and seriousness of hazards that have been discovered. Risks are prioritized according to their importance, urgency, and possible outcomes. Creating risk profiles and heat maps can help you better visualize and explain your exposure to risk.

- **Risk Mitigation and Control:** Putting strategies and controls in place to lessen the chance or effect of hazards that have been recognized to a manageable level. Internal control implementation, risk transfer mechanisms (such as insurance), risk diversification, hedging techniques, contingency planning, and business continuity planning are a few examples of this.

- **Risk Monitoring and Review:** Keeping an eye on the status of hazards that have been identified and tracking it over time to make sure that mitigation strategies are working and risks are being managed within reasonable bounds. reviewing risk management procedures, controls, and tactics on a frequent basis in order to spot new risks, evaluate their viability, and make necessary modifications to account for evolving conditions.

- **Risk Reporting and Communication:** Sharing risk data, evaluations, and mitigation plans with important constituencies, such as the board of directors, senior management, staff, investors, and outside parties. In order to promote responsible and educated decision-making, timely and transparent reporting on risk exposures, trends, and mitigation initiatives should be provided.

Intellectual Property Protection

For organizations to protect their intangible assets—like innovations, creative works, trademarks, and sensitive information—from illegal use, infringement, or misappropriation, intellectual property (IP) protection is essential. Businesses may profit from their inventions, keep a competitive edge, and create value from their intellectual property with the help of IP protection. The following explains how intellectual property is protected in the commercial world:

1. Identical Property Types:

- **Patents:** Give the creator exclusive rights to new items, methods, or technologies for a set amount of time (usually 20 years) in order to protect inventions and innovations. Patents offer legal defense against unapproved production, use, importation, or sale of the patented innovation.

- **Copyrights:** Give the creator or owner exclusive rights to preserve unique works of authorship, such as music, software, architectural designs, literary works, and creative creations. Copyrights prohibit the unapproved duplication, dissemination, exhibition in public, or modification of works protected by copyright.

- **Trademarks:** guard names, emblems, catchphrases, and other distinguishing marks or symbols that are used to identify and set products and services apart in the marketplace. With trademarks, the owner of the mark has the only authority to use, grant licenses, and keep the registered mark safe from infringement or diluting by rivals.

- **Trade Secrets:** Maintain confidentiality and put in place the necessary security measures to safeguard proprietary and sensitive information, such as formulae, recipes, customer lists, production processes, and corporate procedures. Trade secrets offer advantages over competitors and legal defense against theft or unapproved disclosure.

- **Industrial Designs:** Give the creator or owner exclusive rights to preserve the visual appeal or artistic features of goods or designs, such as form, arrangement, embellishment, or pattern. Industrial designs forbid unlawful duplication or emulation of the registered design.

2. Legal Mechanisms for Intellectual Property Protection:

- **Registration:** To establish legal ownership and enforceability of intellectual property rights, obtain official registration or certification of intellectual property rights with government agencies, such as patent offices, copyright offices, trademark offices, or intellectual property offices. Registration makes it easier to take enforcement action against infringers and provides initial proof of ownership.

- **Contracts and Agreements:** In commercial transactions, partnerships, collaborations, and licensing agreements, use contracts, agreements, and licensing arrangements to establish and safeguard intellectual property rights, obligations, and constraints. To make clear the rights and obligations of parties involved, include clauses for confidentiality, non-disclosure, non-compete, and assignment of intellectual property rights.

- **Enforcement and Litigation:** Use civil litigation, administrative procedures, or alternative dispute resolution procedures to bring legal action against those who infringe or violate intellectual property rights. usage cease and desist letters, injunctions, reparations, or settlements to enforce intellectual property rights, put an end to unlawful usage, and seek recompense for any losses or damages suffered.

- **International Treaties and Agreements:** Use international conventions, treaties, and agreements to secure and uphold intellectual property rights internationally. Examples of these include the Agreement on Trade-Related Aspects of Intellectual Property Rights (TRIPS), the Paris Convention for the Protection of Industrial Property, and the Berne Convention for the Protection of Literary and Artistic Works.

3. IP Strategy and Management:

- **IP Portfolio Management:** Create a thorough plan for managing your portfolio of intellectual property in order to find, acquire, safeguard, and capitalize on valuable assets that support your company's aims and objectives. Give strategic value, market uniqueness, and potential for income-generating investments top priority when making investments in intellectual property.

Risk Assessment and Mitigation: To identify possible IP risks, vulnerabilities, and exposures inside the organization, conduct risk assessments and audits. To protect IP assets from risks and vulnerabilities, put risk mitigation techniques into practice. These include IP insurance, monitoring and surveillance, compliance procedures, and cybersecurity measures.

- **Innovation and R&D:** Encourage an innovative, creative, and R&D culture inside the company to produce new concepts, innovations, and technologies that can be patentable and made commercially available. Invest in R&D projects, technology licensing, and patent applications to take advantage of IP possibilities and gain a competitive edge.

- **Partnerships and Collaborations:** To take advantage of complementary intellectual property assets, pool resources, and spur innovation, establish strategic alliances, partnerships, and collaborations with other companies, academic institutions, or technology transfer organizations. Create precise agreements for revenue-sharing, IP ownership, and licensing to minimize disagreements and increase value generation.

- **IP Enforcement and Defense:** Create proactive plans and tactics to protect intellectual property rights from piracy, infringement, and illegal usage. To prevent infringement and safeguard market share, keep an eye out for any IP violations in the marketplace, take enforcement action against infringers, and vigorously defend IP rights through the legal system.

CHAPTER 4

CREATING A WINNING TEAM

Hiring and Retaining Top Talent

Building a high-performing team that fosters innovation and corporate success requires hiring and keeping great personnel. The following actions can help you draw in, select, and keep great talent for your company:

1. Explain Your Talent Requirements and Standards: Determine the precise abilities, credentials, and qualities you are seeking in applicants first. For every position, clearly define the duties, responsibilities, and performance standards. Take into account both hard and soft abilities that complement the principles and culture of your organization.

2. Create an Employer Brand:

Create a compelling employer brand that highlights the culture, values, and distinctive advantages that make your organization a great place to work. Emphasize the advantages of working for your company, such as chances for professional growth, a work-life balance, employee perks, and a supportive work atmosphere.

Enhance your employer brand by utilizing industry awards, employee testimonials, and social media.

3. Deploy a Focused Hiring Approach:

To draw in top talent, use a variety of recruitment strategies and channels, including job boards, university alliances, professional networking sites, employee recommendations, recruitment agencies, and career fairs. Adapt your recruiting approach to target particular industry sectors, applicant demographics, or skill sets that correspond with your talent requirements.

4. Streamline the Hiring Process:

In a competitive employment market, streamline your hiring procedures to draw in and hold on to top talent. Streamline the application process, reduce red tape, and provide applicants with rapid feedback at every stage of the hiring process. ATSs and video interviews are two examples of technologies that may be used to automate and optimize the hiring process.

5. Perform a Comprehensive Candidate Assessment:

Assess candidates' credentials, experience, and cultural fit using a mix of tests, interviews, and reference checks. To evaluate applicants' problem-solving abilities, collaboration, communication, and flexibility, conduct behavioral interviews. Engage a variety of stakeholders in the recruiting process to obtain a range of viewpoints and guarantee alignment with the objectives of the business.

6. Provide competitive benefits and compensation: Offer perks and pay plans that are competitive to draw and keep top workers. To compare compensation, bonuses, and incentives to rivals and industry norms, do market research. Provide extra incentives and advantages, including health insurance, retirement plans, flexible work schedules, chances for professional growth, and wellness initiatives for staff members.

7. Promote career development and growth:

To draw and keep top talent, provide possibilities for growth and development for your staff. Give staff members access to workshops, certifications, training courses, and mentoring opportunities that will improve their knowledge, abilities, and chances for professional progress. Provide unambiguous channels for advancement, recognition, and leadership cultivation inside the establishment.

8. Create a Positive Workplace:

Encourage a workplace where diversity, inclusivity, teamwork, and work-life balance are valued. Foster a culture of gratitude, acknowledgment, and constructive criticism to inspire and involve staff members. To foster loyalty and trust, promote open communication, honesty, and employee empowerment.

9. Offer continuous assistance and acknowledgement:

Employees should be honored for their accomplishments, efforts, and overall performance. Put in place employee recognition initiatives, prizes, and incentives that honor both individual and group achievements. Give staff regular coaching, support, and feedback to ensure they are successful and happy in their positions.

10. Keep an eye on employee satisfaction and engagement:

Utilize performance evaluations, feedback sessions, and surveys to routinely gauge employee happiness and engagement levels. Utilize employee input to pinpoint areas in need of development, handle issues, and carry out programs that boost morale, output, and retention.

Fostering a Positive Company Culture

In order to create a helpful, welcoming, and stimulating work environment where workers feel appreciated, inspired, and empowered to give their all, it is imperative to cultivate a good business culture. The following are some tactics to promote a positive workplace culture:

1. Define and Communicate Core Values:

Clearly define your organization's fundamental values so that they represent the attitudes, values, and conduct you would like to see promoted. Use frequent communication channels, such as corporate meetings, newsletters, the intranet, and signage, to successfully convey these principles to the workforce. For your organization's choices, activities, and policies to be more significant and applicable, make sure they are in line with your fundamental values.

2. Lead by Example:

Set an example of leadership by acting in ways that reflect the ideals and tenets of your company's culture. Establish a good tone at the top by acting with honesty, humility, openness, and respect while interacting with stakeholders, customers, and staff. To build confidence and trust among your team, communicate and make decisions in an honest, personable, and sympathetic manner.

3. Promote Open Communication:

Establish an environment where staff members are at ease discussing thoughts, opinions, worries, and recommendations with peers and management. To encourage two-way communication and cooperation, set up a variety of venues for communication, including employee forums, town hall meetings, suggestion boxes, and digital platforms. Encourage workers to participate in decision-making processes that impact them, actively listen to their views, and swiftly resolve any issues they may have.

4. Promote Collaboration and Teamwork:

Encourage a cooperative workplace where staff members cooperate between departments, teams, and functions to accomplish shared goals and objectives. Promote cooperation, creativity, and group problem-solving by supporting efforts for knowledge sharing, team-building, and cross-functional projects. To reinforce desired actions and outcomes, acknowledge and praise collaboration and teamwork.

5. Encourage a work-life balance:

Encourage work-life balance by providing flexible work arrangements that take into account employees' personal and professional obligations, such as reduced workweeks, flexible scheduling, and remote work possibilities. Encourage staff members to take frequent vacations, breaks, and time off in order to refuel. Offer tools and assistance to achieve work-life balance, wellbeing, and stress management.

6. Invest in the Training of Staff: Put employee development and growth first by giving them access to coaching, certifications, workshops, seminars, and training programs that will improve their knowledge, abilities, and chances for professional success. Provide workers with individualized development plans and career trajectories to facilitate their advancement inside the company and in their careers.

7. Promote Diversity and Inclusion:

Make diversity and inclusion a central part of your company's culture and cultivate a work atmosphere where staff members feel appreciated, respected, and part of the team regardless of their differences, identities, or backgrounds. To foster a culture of fairness and belonging, put diversity and inclusion initiatives—like affinity groups, mentoring programs, training on unconscious bias, and diversity recruiting efforts—into action.

8. Acknowledge and Value Workers:

Recognize and value staff members' accomplishments, efforts, and contributions by holding frequent awards ceremonies, recognition programs, and incentive drives. To express gratitude and encourage constructive behavior, publicly and privately recognize and celebrate team and individual successes. Give staff constructive criticism and recognition for exceptional work to spur them on to keep doing their best work.

9. Advocate for Health and Welfare:

Make employee health and well-being a priority by providing tools, health initiatives, and wellness programs that promote mental, emotional, and physical health. To assist staff in maintaining a good work-life balance and learning effective coping mechanisms for stress, make fitness centers, mindfulness exercises, counseling services, and wellness courses accessible to them.

10. Celebrate Company Traditions and Rituals:

Establish and preserve events, customs, and rituals that give staff members a feeling of pride, community, and belonging. Plan social gatherings, holiday parties, milestone anniversaries, and team-building exercises to foster relationships, fortify bonds, and provide treasured moments that enhance the business culture.

Leadership Development and Empowerment

Establishing a solid company culture and promoting commercial success require enhanced leadership and empowerment. Here are some ideas for encouraging empowerment and leadership development in your company:

1. Find and Develop Future Leaders:

Recognize personnel with high potential who exhibit initiative, leadership potential, and a growth mentality. Provide them the chance to grow as leaders through training programs, coaching, mentorship, and stretch assignments that force them to acquire new talents, viewpoints, and skills. To promote both professional and personal development, encourage never-ending learning and self-improvement.

2. Cultivate a Growth Mindset:

Encourage staff members to take on challenges, grow from mistakes, and persevere in the face of obstacles.

Establish a culture that rewards and values experimentation, creativity, and learning. Encourage employees to improve their resilience, flexibility, and growth-oriented mindset by giving them constructive criticism and encouragement.

3. Offer Programs for Leadership Development and Training:

Provide thorough leadership development and training programs that provide staff members with the abilities, know-how, and competencies necessary to be successful leaders. Cover subjects like decision-making, conflict resolution, communication, emotional intelligence, strategic thinking, and change management. Offer chances for practical experience, role-playing, and practical application to strengthen learning and skill development.

4. Promote ownership and accountability:

Provide staff members with the freedom, authority, and capacity to make decisions so they can accept responsibility for their work, projects, and duties. Motivate them to take initiative, establish ambitious objectives, and come up with original solutions to issues. Hold staff members responsible for their actions and outcomes while offering them the resources, support, and direction they need to be successful.

5. Lead by Example:

Showcase successful leadership techniques and actions that encourage, uplift, and give people authority. Set a good example for others to follow by acting with honesty, decency, humility, and compassion for your coworkers. Give aspiring leaders assistance, direction, and mentoring so they may assume leadership positions and responsibilities.

6. Create a Culture of Trust and Collaboration:

Encourage an environment where workers feel appreciated, respected, and free to express any thoughts, issues, or opinions. Establish open lines of communication, promote discussion and criticism, and include staff members in decisions that have an impact on them. Establish trusting bonds and encourage cooperation among staff members to establish a welcoming and inclusive workplace.

7. Acknowledge and Honor Leadership Achievements:

Acknowledge and honor staff members who show initiative, leadership, and success-oriented contributions to the company. Celebrate leadership excellence, accomplishments, and landmarks with official recognition programs, prizes, and incentives. Offer prospects for professional growth, job promotions, and leadership positions to staff members who exhibit leadership abilities and achievements.

8. Furnish Constant Education and Advancement:

Establish a culture of lifelong learning and growth where staff members are motivated to take on new tasks, learn new abilities, and look for chances for personal improvement. Give people access to learning opportunities, tools, and resources that promote empowerment and leadership development, such as conferences, workshops, seminars, online courses, and coaching programs.

9. Promote Diversity and Inclusion:

Embrace a range of viewpoints, experiences, and backgrounds to promote diversity and inclusion inside your company. Provide your diverse workforce the chance to engage in leadership development initiatives, mentorship programs, and career growth possibilities. Encourage an inclusive culture in which each person is encouraged to share their special skills and viewpoints and feels appreciated, respected, and empowered to do so.

10. Evaluate and Measure Leadership Effectiveness: Keep assessing and measuring how well your programs for empowerment and leadership development are working. To evaluate the performance, impact, and efficacy of your leadership, get input from peers, colleagues, and superiors. Utilize metrics, evaluations, and performance reviews to monitor advancement, pinpoint problem areas, and gradually enhance your leadership development techniques.

CHAPTER 5

MARKETING AND SALES STRATEGIES

Market Research and Target Audience Analysis

In order to create a marketing plan that successfully reaches and interacts with your target audience, market research and target audience analysis are essential. Here's how to evaluate your target audience and carry out market research:

1. Explain Your Goals:

Establish the goals of your target audience analysis and market research in explicit terms first. To properly guide your marketing plan, decide what particular information you need to collect, such as market trends, consumer preferences, competition research, or demographic data.

2. Identify Your Target Market:

Describe your ideal clientele by pinpointing their precise demographic, geographic, psychographic, and behavioral traits. To build comprehensive customer personas that accurately reflect your target audience groups, take into account variables like age, gender, income, education, lifestyle, hobbies, values, and pain points.

3. Conduct Market Research:

Use a variety of research techniques, such as the following, to compile information and insights about your market, rivals, industry, and consumer preferences.

- **Desk Research:** To obtain a comprehensive grasp of market dynamics, trends, and the competitive landscape, gather secondary data from industry reports, market studies, university research, government publications, and internet sources.

- **Questionnaires and Surveys:** Create and disseminate questionnaires or surveys to collect first-hand information from your intended audience. Customers and prospects can provide comments, thoughts, and insights through in-person interviews, email marketing, social media platforms, and online survey tools.

- **Focus Groups:** To investigate attitudes, perceptions, motives, and preferences pertaining to your goods, services, or brand, arrange focus groups or qualitative research sessions with a chosen set of participants. To find important ideas, lead conversations, pose insightful questions, and watch participant replies.

- **Competitor Analysis:** To find opportunities, threats, and points of distinction from the competition, examine your rivals' offerings, pricing, distribution methods, marketing plans, strengths, and weaknesses. Compare your performance to those of your main rivals and industry standards to find areas where you may improve.

- **Trend Analysis:** Keep an eye out for developments that might affect your company and the market, such as macroeconomic issues, consumer behavior patterns, technological breakthroughs, and changes in regulations. Keep up with new trends and developments in the industry to be able to predict changes and modify your marketing plan as necessary.

4. Analyze and Interpret Data:

Examine the information gathered from your market research projects in order to pinpoint important discoveries, patterns, trends, and business prospects. To glean insightful information from your data, apply both quantitative and qualitative analytic approaches, such as sentiment analysis, data visualization, statistical analysis, and theme coding. Seek out patterns, connections, and anomalies that might guide your choices for marketing strategy.

5. Develop Customer Personas:

Create thorough customer personas that accurately reflect your ideal clients using the data you obtained from your target audience investigation. Create discrete personas for your target audience according to their behavioral, psychographic, and demographic traits. To construct extensive and complex client profiles, include details like age, gender, income, preferences, pain areas, **objectives, problems, and reasons for purchasing.**

6. Optimize Your Promotional Approach:

Refine your marketing plan and methods by using the information from your target audience analysis and market research. To better connect with your target audience groups, customize your messaging, branding, product offers, price, distribution methods, and promotional activities. Create content and marketing campaigns that are specifically tailored to each consumer's requirements, interests, and preferences.

7. Monitor and evaluate performance:

Keep a close eye on the results of your marketing campaigns to gauge how well they're connecting with and reaching your target market. To gauge the success of your marketing initiatives, monitor key performance indicators (KPIs), including website traffic, conversion rates, measures for customer engagement, sales revenue, and return on investment (ROI). To assign results to certain marketing channels and activities and adjust your marketing strategy appropriately, use data analytics and marketing attribution models.

Crafting Compelling Marketing Messages

In order to grab your target audience's attention, speak to their wants and aspirations, and inspire them to act, you must craft persuasive marketing communications. To assist you in creating effective marketing messaging, follow these steps:

1. Know Who Your Audience Is:

Begin by comprehending the characteristics, inclinations, problems, and goals of your target market. Utilize customer surveys, market research, and persona building to learn more about the factors that drive and impact the decisions made by your target audience.

2. Emphasize Advantages, Not Features:

Rather than merely stating the details of your product or service, concentrate on emphasizing its advantages. Make it obvious how your product or service meets a need, solves an issue, or meaningfully enhances the lives of those it serves. Demonstrate to them how your offering may improve, ease, or add enjoyment to their lives.

3. Appeal to Emotions:

Consumer behavior can be significantly influenced by emotional appeal. To connect with your audience, craft messages that arouse feelings like joy, excitement, fear, pride, or empathy. To arouse feelings in your audience and establish a stronger connection, use realistic events, vivid imagery, and narrative.

4. Use persuasive language:

To change your audience's mind and behavior, use persuasive language and persuasive strategies. Make use of language that conveys a sense of exclusivity, urgency, scarcity, or social proof. Emphasize the advantages, features, or inducements—like time-limited deals, freebies, discounts, or guarantees—that will persuade your audience to act.

5. Be clear and succinct:

Make sure your marketing communications are clear, succinct, and easy to grasp. Steer clear of jargon, technical terms, and needless intricacy that might turn off or confuse your readers. Make use of clear, concise language to deliver your point swiftly and successfully.

6. Differentiate Your Brand:

Set yourself apart from the competition by emphasizing the qualities that make you special. Make a strong case for your brand's value proposition, distinctive selling features, and competitive advantages. Demonstrate to your audience your superiority over competitors and why you are the best option for their needs.

7. Tailor Messages to Each Audience Segment:

Divide your audience into groups according to their characteristics, interests, or habits, then craft messages that speak to each group. Make sure your messaging is tailored to each target segment's unique wants, interests, and pain areas to give them the impression that you appreciate and comprehend their unique demands.

8. Use Visuals to Enhance Your Message:

Use visuals to improve and make your marketing messaging more memorable and engaging. Examples of these are photos, videos, infographics, and graphics.

Make use of images that visually appeal to the eye, amplify your message, or highlight the advantages of your item or service.

9. Contain an Unambiguous Call-to-Action (CTA):

In order to encourage your audience to take the desired action—such as making a purchase, subscribing to a newsletter, seeking more information, or following you on social media—you should always include a call-to-action (CTA) in your marketing messaging that is both clear and engaging. Use clear instructions and action-oriented language to make your call to action (CTA) stand out and be easy to respond to.

10. Test and iterate:

To maximize the impact and efficacy of your marketing communications, test and refine them often. To find out which headlines, graphics, CTAs, or message variants work best with your audience, A/B test them all. Examine the outcomes and comments, and utilize the information gained to gradually enhance and strengthen your messaging.

Building Effective Sales Funnels

To help prospective consumers go from early awareness to making a purchase decision, it is essential to build efficient sales funnels. To increase conversions and boost income, follow these steps for building and refining a sales funnel:

1. Identify the Stages of Your Sales Funnel:

Start by outlining the phases of your sales funnel, from awareness to conversion, in accordance with the customer journey. Typical phases consist of:

- **Awareness:** drawing in prospective clients and educating them about your company, goods, and services.

- **Interest:** Nurturing interest in prospects by interacting with them and offering insightful material or information.

- **Decision:** By emphasizing the advantages and worth of your service, you may assist prospects in weighing their alternatives and coming to a purchase decision.

- **Action:** Pressuring potential customers to take a certain action, like buying something, joining a trial, or asking for further details.

2. Identify Audience Segments of Interest:

Divide up the people in your target market according to their characteristics, habits, hobbies, or purchasing habits. Make sure that your offerings, content, and message are customized to each target segment's **unique demands and concerns.**

- **Construct attractive offers and content:** Create offers and content of the highest caliber that will appeal to your target market at every point in the sales funnel. Address their queries, worries, or objections by offering helpful resources, information, and solutions. To engage prospects and advance them down the funnel, use a variety of content formats, including eBooks, webinars, videos, case studies, blog entries, and product demos.

3. Maximize Conversion Points and Landing Pages:

Create landing pages and conversion points that are optimized to lead leads through the sales funnel and motivate them to proceed. To elicit action and increase conversions, use attention-grabbing headlines, persuasive copywriting, persuasive images, and obvious calls-to-action (CTAs). Minimize friction and increase conversions by keeping forms and checkout procedures straightforward and well-organized.

4. Implement Strategies for Lead Capture and Nurturing:

At different stages in the sales funnel, collect leads by providing opt-in forms, lead magnets, or gated content that catches prospects' attention. Utilize marketing automation, email marketing, and customized follow-up campaigns to cultivate leads gradually and maintain awareness. Offers, updates, and pertinent information to keep prospects interested and in the process of converting.

5. Track and Measure Performance:

Track the effectiveness of your sales funnel and pinpoint areas for development by using analytics and tracking solutions. Keep an eye on important data like lead quality, time on page, conversion rates, bounce rates, and traffic sources. To maximize outcomes, improve funnel components, including messaging, design, offers, and call to action (CTAs), using A/B testing and experimentation.

6. Optimize for Mobile and User Experience:

Make sure your sales funnel offers a consistent user experience on all platforms and devices and is optimized for mobile. To accommodate mobile users and lower bounce rates, employ mobile-friendly layouts, responsive design, and quickly loaded sites. To make sure your funnel is accessible and user-friendly, test it across a range of devices and screen sizes.

7. Provide social proof and trust signals:

Throughout your sales funnel, display social proof, client recommendations, reviews, ratings, and trust badges to help prospects gain confidence and trust. To reassure prospects and dispel doubts, highlight success stories and excellent customer experiences. Strategically use social proof to increase trust and credibility in your company and products.

8. Offer Incentives and Discounts:

Encourage prospects to take action and advance through the sales funnel by offering incentives, discounts, promotions, or time-limited deals. To entice potential customers to buy or proceed, provide exclusive discounts, free trials, incentives, or special offers. Establish a sense of scarcity or urgency to elicit quick action and increase conversions.

9. Continuously Iterate and Improve:

Evaluate and track your sales funnel's effectiveness on a regular basis. Then, make data-driven changes to enhance outcomes over time. To improve the overall efficacy of your sales funnel, minimize friction points, and maximize conversion rates, test various approaches, methods, and messaging variants. React quickly and sensitively to shifting consumer tastes, market conditions, and rivalry dynamics.

CHAPTER 6

HARNESSING TECHNOLOGY FOR GROWTH

Leveraging Digital Tools and Platforms

Utilizing technology-driven solutions and online platforms to accomplish a range of corporate goals, including marketing, sales, customer service, operations, and collaboration, is known as "leveraging digital tools and platforms." Through the use of these tools and platforms, organizations may increase consumer interaction, reach a larger audience, streamline procedures, and foster efficiency and creativity. Below is a summary of the various ways in which businesses might use digital tools and platforms:

1. Marketing and Advertising:

- **Social Media Marketing:** Post content, manage advertising campaigns, and increase brand recognition by interacting with target audiences on social media sites like Facebook, Instagram, Twitter, LinkedIn, and YouTube.

- **Search Engine Optimization (SEO):** Through search engines like Google, Bing, and Yahoo, optimize your website's content and structure to increase search engine ranks and exposure, drive organic traffic, and draw in qualified leads.

- **Email Marketing:** To nurture leads, advertise goods and services, and increase conversions, use email marketing systems to design and deliver newsletters, automated sequences, and targeted email campaigns.

- **Content Marketing:** Produce and disseminate informative, engaging, and valuable content—blog entries, articles, podcasts, videos, infographics, and eBooks—to draw in readers and establish authority for your brand.

2. Sales and E-commerce:

- **E-commerce Platforms:** Use platforms like Shopify, WooCommerce, Magento, or BigCommerce to set up and manage online storefronts and e-commerce websites in order to sell goods and services to clients directly.

- **Customer Relationship Management (CRM):** Use CRM programs like HubSpot, Zoho CRM, or Salesforce to automate sales processes, manage leads and contacts, track customer interactions, and analyze customer data for insights and tailored communications.

- **Sales Enablement Tools:** To improve lead prioritization, streamline sales processes, and boost sales performance, arm sales teams with tools and resources including email tracking, lead scoring, sales automation software, and predictive analytics.

3. Client Care and Assistance:

- **Help Desk and Ticketing Systems:** Use help desk software like Zendesk, Freshdesk, or Help Scout to effectively handle client questions, support tickets, and service requests and offer prompt answers and solutions.**Live Chat and Chatbots:** Use AI-powered chatbots or live chat platforms connected to websites, mobile applications, or messaging channels to deliver real-time customer support and help. Respond to consumer inquiries, provide information, and quickly resolve issues.

- **Self-Service Portals:** Establish digitally available self-service knowledge bases, FAQs, tutorials, and user manuals that enable clients to autonomously solve issues and discover solutions to frequently asked queries.

4. Operations and Productivity:

- **Project Management Tools:** Plan, arrange, and monitor projects, tasks, and deadlines; interact with team members; and effectively manage workflows by utilizing project management platforms such as Asana, Trello, or Basecamp.

- **Collaboration Software:** Use tools like Slack, Microsoft Teams, or Google Workspace to facilitate communication and collaboration among team members remotely. These platforms allow for real-time chat, file sharing, video conferencing, and document collaboration.

- **Workflow Automation:** To automate repetitive operations, link applications and systems, and optimize business processes across departments and functions, use workflow automation technologies like Microsoft Power Automate, Integromat, or Zapier.

5. Analytics and Insights:

- **Web Analytics:** Track website traffic, user behavior, conversion rates, and other key performance indicators (KPIs) to gauge the success of digital marketing campaigns and website performance. You can do this by using web analytics platforms like Google Analytics, Adobe Analytics, or Matomo.

- **Social Media Analytics:** To improve social media strategies and campaigns, track and evaluate social media metrics, engagement, sentiment, and audience demographics using social media analytics tools and insights from platforms like Facebook Insights, Twitter Analytics, or LinkedIn Analytics.

- **Corporate Intelligence (BI):** To display, analyze, and understand corporate data, create reports, and unearth actionable insights to guide strategic planning and decision-making, utilize BI tools and dashboards like Tableau, Microsoft Power BI, or Google Data Studio.

Automation and Streamlining Processes

Process automation and streamlining refer to the use of technology and effective workflows to minimize manual involvement, automate repetitive activities, and optimize operations for higher levels of productivity, cost-effectiveness, and efficiency. Here are some strategies that companies may use to take advantage of automation and optimize certain processes:

1. Identify bottlenecks and repetitive tasks:

Begin by determining whether procedures and tasks are time-consuming, error-prone, repetitious, or prone to bottlenecks. To find inefficiencies, duplications, and pain spots in current processes, do workflow analysis, process audits, and stakeholder interviews.

2. Evaluate Automation Opportunities:

Consider the intricacy, regularity, and effect of jobs and procedures on corporate operations when evaluating automation prospects. To increase productivity, accuracy, and scalability, identify whether jobs may be automated with software tools, robotic process automation (RPA), or technology.

3. Choose the Right Automation Tools:

Select automation technologies and tools that fit your budget, objectives, and expectations as a firm. Investigate a range of automation options, including low-code and no-code platforms, artificial intelligence (AI), machine learning (ML), business process management (BPM) software, RPA tools, and workflow automation platforms.

4. Implement Workflow Automation:

To improve and simplify repetitive operations and procedures across departments and functions, implement workflow automation solutions. Reduce manual labor and increase operational efficiency by automating processes including data input, document processing, form submissions, approvals, alerts, **reminders, and scheduling.**

5. Integrate Systems and Applications:

To facilitate smooth data flow and communication across various systems and departments, integrate dissimilar systems, applications, and data sources. For increased automation and interoperability, link databases, cloud apps, third-party services, and legacy systems using integration tools, APIs, middleware, and connectors.

6. Standardize Processes and Workflows:

Create uniform, replicable, and expandable procedures throughout the company by standardizing processes and workflows. To clearly outline expectations, roles, and handoffs for every stage of the process, document standard operating procedures (SOPs), workflow diagrams, and process maps.

7. Promote Collaboration and Self-Service:

Provide self-service tools, portals, and platforms to employees and stakeholders so they can work together, access information, and start activities without needing human assistance. To lessen workload and increase response, provide self-service solutions for things like IT assistance, HR questions, procurement requests, and customer service inquiries.

8. Monitor and Measure Performance:

Use analytics, metrics, and key performance indicators (KPIs) to track and evaluate the effectiveness of automated processes and workflows. To evaluate the efficiency and return on investment (ROI) of automation projects, monitor parameters including process cycle time, throughput, mistake rates, resource utilization, and cost reductions.

9. Continuously Improve and Optimize:

Based on input, understanding, and lessons gained, continuously iterate and improve automated processes and workflows. Seek feedback from users, stakeholders, and process owners in order to pinpoint areas that require innovation, optimization, and improvement. Over time, increase efficiency, effectiveness, and value by putting updates, upgrades, and refinements into practice.

10. Assure Compliance and Security:

Verify that automated workflows and procedures abide by industry norms, legal requirements, and security best practices. Protect sensitive data, preserve data privacy, and reduce security risks related to automation by putting in place audit trails, monitoring systems, access limits, and data encryption.

Data Analytics for Informed Decision-Making

In order to find insights, patterns, trends, and correlations that guide company strategy and decision-making, data analytics entails gathering, analyzing, interpreting, and visualizing data. The following are some ways that data analytics may help firms make well-informed decisions:

1. Data Gathering and Combination:

Begin by gathering information from a variety of sources, including social media, sensors, online traffic, marketing campaigns, transactional systems, and third-party sources. Gather information from several sources and combine it into a single data warehouse or repository for analysis.

2. Data Preparation and Cleaning:

Make sure that the data is accurate, comprehensive, consistent, and of high quality by cleaning, validating, and preprocessing it. Use methods like data imputation, normalization, and outlier identification to deal with duplicates, inconsistencies, missing values, and outliers in the data. The data should be formatted and transformed into a structured format that can be analyzed.

3. Descriptive Analytics:

To summarize and characterize past data patterns, trends, and attributes, apply descriptive analytics approaches. Create histograms, heatmaps, charts, graphs, summary statistics, and visualizations to investigate and comprehend the distribution, variability, and relationships in the data.

4. Diagnostic Analytics:

Use diagnostic analytics to find the underlying causes of abnormalities, historical occurrences, or problems with performance. Use regression analysis, hypothesis testing, and root cause analysis to identify the variables influencing particular results or deviations from expected norms. Determine the correlations, patterns, and connections among the variables that account for the occurrences you have seen.

5. Predictive Analytics:

Using statistical models and past data patterns, apply predictive analytics approaches to estimate future trends, behaviors, or results. To forecast customer behavior, demand, sales, churn, risk, and other important indicators, use forecasting techniques, machine learning algorithms, predictive modeling, and time series analysis. To help you make decisions and predict future occurrences, create forecasts, projections, and predictive scores.

6. Prescriptive Analytics:

Apply prescriptive analytics to suggest the best decisions or courses of action in light of limits, goals, constraints, and prediction models. To assess many situations, trade-offs, and possible outcomes, use simulation models, decision trees, and optimization algorithms. Provide suggestions, decision-support tools, and actionable insights to help decision-makers choose the best course of action.

7. Data Visualization and Reporting:

Make use of data visualization strategies and reporting technologies to communicate insights and discoveries from data analytics in an understandable, user-friendly, and aesthetically pleasing way. Provide interactive visualizations, reports, and dashboards that efficiently convey important data, trends, and insights to stakeholders. Employ interactive tools, maps, infographics, charts, and graphs to help communicate complicated information and support data-driven decision-making.

8. Real-time Analytics and Monitoring:

Put real-time analytics and monitoring tools to use by tracking and analyzing data almost instantly to find trends, patterns, and anomalies as they appear. To keep an eye on operational metrics, business events, and key performance indicators (KPIs) in real time, use event processing, streaming analytics, and real-time dashboards. Facilitate prompt and informed decision-making and action through the use of alerts and insights.

9. Data Governance and Security:

To guarantee the security, privacy, correctness, and integrity of data used for analytics, set up data governance rules, standards, and procedures. Put in place data access restrictions, encryption, masking, and anonymization strategies to safeguard confidential information and adhere to legal mandates. Encourage the organization to adopt a culture of data stewardship, accountability, and moral data usage.

10. Continuous Improvement and Optimization:

Keep an eye on and assess how well data analytics projects are guiding decisions and producing business results. Analyze how analytics projects affect ROI, strategic objectives, and key performance indicators (KPIs). Seek input from users, decision-makers, and stakeholders to find areas where data analytics procedures may be optimized, innovated, and improved.

CHAPTER 7

SCALING YOUR BUSINESS FOR SUCCESS

Expansion Strategies and Opportunities

In order to boost market presence, boost revenue, and establish a long-lasting competitive edge, businesses must identify and pursue growth, scalability, and diversification options. The following are some typical methods and avenues for business expansion:

1. Market Penetration:

Expand market share by entering new market segments or selling more of the company's present offerings to existing clients. Increase sales areas, retail sites, or distribution routes to reach a larger client base and enhance accessibility. Launch marketing campaigns, sales, or loyalty plans to draw in new clients and promote recurring business.

2. Product Development:

Create new goods or services in response to changing consumer demands, inclinations, or market trends. improve upon current goods or services by adding new features, enhancing technology, improving quality, or introducing innovative ideas.

Increase product offerings by branching out into supplemental services or adjacent product categories that support the main business.

3. Market Development:

Expand the client base and seize fresh growth prospects by venturing into new geographic markets, regions, or nations.

Use specialized goods, services, or marketing techniques to reach underrepresented or niche market segments. Modify goods or services to satisfy particular requirements, inclinations, or cultural variances in global marketplaces.

4. Diversification:

To distribute risk and take advantage of fresh development prospects, investigate diversification techniques by venturing into new company lines, industries, or market segments. Enter adjacent markets or verticals that make use of current resources, synergies, or skills to pursue relevant diversification.

Take into account unconnected diversification by venturing into wholly unexplored markets or disruptive chances by entering completely new businesses or sectors.

5. Partnerships and Alliances:

Create joint ventures, alliances, or strategic partnerships with other companies, groups, or stakeholders in order to take advantage of complementary resources, distribution routes, or capabilities. Work together to develop creative solutions, increase market reach, or enhance supply chain efficiency with distributors, suppliers, or industry partners.

Create co-branding projects, franchise partnerships, or licensing agreements to increase brand awareness and penetrate new markets.

6. Acquisitions and Mergers:

Look for M&A opportunities to buy complementary companies, technology, or assets that improve performance, broaden market reach, or spur development.

Determine prospective merger or acquisition candidates who meet the financial, cultural, and strategic fit requirements.

Easily integrate acquired businesses or assets to

maximize synergies, streamline processes, and spur value development.

7. E-commerce and Digital Expansion:

To increase reach, accessibility, and consumer involvement in the digital marketplace, embrace e-commerce and digital platforms. Make investments in online advertising, social media, and digital marketing to draw in and keep consumers using various digital touchpoints. Create omnichannel strategies that combine online and physical channels to offer a unified, smooth experience for customers.

8. Franchising and Licensing:

To duplicate success and enter new markets or regions, franchise already-existing company ideas, concepts, or brands.

Grant licenses to third parties for intellectual property, trademarks, or exclusive technologies in exchange for payments, royalties, or revenue-sharing plans. Assure brand consistency, quality standards, and operational excellence by offering franchisees or licensees training, support, and continuing advice.

9. Corporate Social Responsibility (CSR) and Sustainability:

Look for ways to implement ethical business practices and sustainable growth that meet environmental, social, and governance (ESG) standards.

Incorporate eco-friendly procedures, CSR activities, or sustainability initiatives into business operations to improve brand reputation, draw in ethical customers, and create long-term value.

Make investments in green technology, ethical supplier chains, renewable energy, and circular economy models to reduce your influence on the environment and encourage social responsibility.

10. Internationalization and Global Expansion:

Take advantage of chances for worldwide expansion, diversify income sources, and reach new clientele by entering foreign marketplaces.

Perform market research, evaluate obstacles to market entrance, and create entry plans that are specific to the legal, cultural, and competitive environments of each target market.

Create local presence, alliances, or distribution networks in foreign markets to successfully negotiate cultural quirks, legal constraints, and market dynamics.

Managing Growth Challenges

Strategic planning, proactive decision-making, and efficient execution are necessary for managing growth difficulties in a company in order to avoid possible roadblocks and maintain momentum. The following are some methods for dealing with typical development obstacles:

1. Scale Operations Efficiently:

Examine the systems, procedures, and resources in place to find any inefficiencies, bottlenecks, or capacity restrictions that could prevent expansion. To improve productivity, accommodate expanding needs, and streamline operations, invest in scalable infrastructure, automation, and technology. Use lean techniques, agile approaches, and continuous improvement programs to streamline processes, cut down on waste, and boost agility.

2. Fortify Financial Management:

Create strong cash flow management, budgeting, and financial forecasting procedures to foresee and control the financial risks related to expansion. Track company performance and spot any financial difficulties by keeping an eye on profitability ratios, important financial data, and performance indicators. Find new financial sources to support working capital needs and expansion ambitions, such as loan financing, equity financing, or strategic partnerships.

3. Build and Empower Teams:

Find, hire, and train a diverse, talented staff that can spur innovation and growth at all organizational levels. Encourage employee involvement, initiative, and ownership by fostering a culture of empowerment, accountability, and teamwork. Offer workers professional development opportunities, mentorship, and training to give them the tools, resources, and know-how they need to thrive in a changing and dynamic workplace.

4. Maintain Customer Focus:

Put customer satisfaction, loyalty, and retention first by providing outstanding products, services, and experiences that either meet or surpass customer expectations; Ask for feedback, pay attention to what customers need, and modify products, services, and processes in light of what customers have to say. Make investments in customer relationship management (CRM) systems, customer support channels, and tailored marketing strategies to build and strengthen relationships with customers.

5. Manage Risks and Uncertainty:

Carry out in-depth risk assessments in order to recognize, rank, and reduce any risks and uncertainties related to expansion plans, market conditions, legal modifications, or outside influences. Create backup plans, methods for reducing risks, and crisis management procedures to deal with unanticipated difficulties, interruptions, or downturns. Diversify your income sources, clientele, and geographical markets to lessen your reliance on any one industry or revenue stream.

6. Adapt and Innovate:

Promote an innovative, experimental, and flexible culture that stimulates innovative thinking, problem-solving, and agility in response to shifting market conditions. Keep up with emerging technologies, industry trends, and competitive dynamics to spot opportunities for innovation, disruption, and differentiation. Promote cooperation, cross-functional teamwork, and idea-sharing to ignite innovation and propel continuous improvement across the entire organization.

7. Maintain Strategic Focus:

Pursue development prospects, expansion projects, and strategic alliances while being loyal to the organization's purpose, vision, and fundamental values. Give top priority to expansion projects and capital expenditures that are in line with competitive positioning, long-term strategic goals, and sustainable value generation.

Apply a strategic lens to assess prospective opportunities and challenges, taking into account how they may affect the entire business strategy, profitability, and competitive advantage.

Building Scalable Systems and Processes

Businesses must have scalable systems and procedures in order to handle expansion, boost productivity, and adjust to shifting needs. Businesses can create scalable systems and procedures in the following ways:

1. Evaluate Existing Procedures:

To begin with, assess current processes, systems, and workflows in order to pinpoint inefficiencies, bottlenecks, and opportunities for enhancement. To comprehend the inputs, outputs, relationships, and pain points of each process, document and analyze it.

2. Standardize and Simplify:

To guarantee uniformity, repeatability, and scalability, standardize procedures throughout the company. Reduce the number of manual stages, get rid of pointless chores, and simplify complicated operations.

3. Automate repetitive processes:

Reduce the need for manual intervention and minimize mistakes by streamlining and automating repetitive processes with the use of technology and automation tools. To automate repetitive tasks and free up resources for higher-value tasks, use software solutions, robotic process automation (RPA), and workflow automation.

4. Design for Flexibility and Adaptability:

To account for expansion, demand fluctuations, and changing company needs, systems and procedures should be designed with flexibility and adaptability in mind. Construct modular parts, flexible workflows, and scalable systems that are easy to scale up or down in response to demands.

5. Invest in Scalable Technology:

Make an investment in software, platforms, and scalable technological infrastructure to support expanding business operations. Select modular programs that can extend dynamically to accommodate rising workloads, scalable databases, and cloud-based solutions.

6. Apply Agile Approaches:

Adopt agile approaches like Scrum or Kanban to encourage quick requirement adaptation, iterative development, and continuous improvement. Divide large jobs into smaller, more manageable ones, rank the work according to its importance, and iterate in response to input and new information.

7. Create Teams That Work Together:

Encourage cooperation and cross-functional teamwork by dismantling organizational silos and assembling people with a range of knowledge and experience. Form interdisciplinary teams capable of collaborating to find innovative solutions to challenging issues and advance process enhancements.

8. Monitor Performance and Metrics:

To gauge the effectiveness and scalability of systems and procedures, define metrics and key performance indicators (KPIs). To find areas for improvement and performance bottlenecks, track measures like throughput, cycle time, reaction time, and resource use.

9. Continuous Improvement:

Encourage staff members to find and apply process improvements in order to promote a culture of learning and continuous improvement. To reflect on accomplishments, setbacks, and lessons learned, set up feedback loops, post-mortems, and periodical retrospectives. Then, incorporate input into subsequent versions.

10. Document and Train:

To guarantee uniformity and promote knowledge sharing, document best practices, standardized procedures, and workflows. Employees should get continuing assistance, training, and onboarding to make sure they comprehend and adhere to established protocols.

11. Plan for Scalability:

When developing systems and procedures, take future expansion and scalability requirements into account. Planning for infrastructure, resource allocation, and capacity management should take into account variables including projected business growth, seasonal variations, and market trends.

12. Test Scalability:

To evaluate how systems and processes function under various loads and circumstances, do performance and scalability tests. To replicate real-world situations and spot possible bottlenecks or limits, use load testing, stress testing, and scalability testing techniques.

CONCLUSION

Finally, "How to Make Your Business Your Business" offers a thorough manual for negotiating the challenges of entrepreneurship and creating a profitable company from the ground up. We have covered a wide range of important subjects in this book, such as creating a strong business plan, managing cash flow, investing sensibly, and comprehending legal requirements. We also looked at how important it is to set clear goals and objectives, cultivate a positive workplace culture, and support leadership development in order to empower teams and propel organizational growth. Finally, we have covered the importance of market research, target audience analysis, and creating persuasive marketing messages to draw in and keep clients in a competitive market.

Furthermore, the book emphasizes the importance of data analytics in informed decision-making, scaling, and continual improvement. In today's changing business environment, firms may maintain momentum, manage operations, and respond to growth problems by utilizing automation, optimizing processes, and developing scalable systems.

In the end, "How to Make Your Business Your Business" is a helpful tool for professionals in the business world as well as those who are just starting out. It provides useful advice, doable tactics, and real-world examples to encourage and mentor readers as they embark on their entrepreneurial journey. Through hard work, determination, and a strategic mindset, people can turn their ideas for their businesses into reality and succeed in the dynamic business environment.

www.ingramcontent.com/pod-product-compliance
Lightning Source LLC
Chambersburg PA
CBHW050040260726

48658CB00005B/1691